THE COMPLETE GUIDE TO
SOCIAL SECURITY DISABILITY

How to Qualify, Apply, and Maximize Your SSI, SSDI, and State Benefits

JUDITH WHITE-LARKINS
and Michael D. Moore

The Complete Guide to Social Security Disability
How to Qualify, Apply, and Maximize Your SSI, SSDI, and State Benefits

Moore-White-Larkins Publishing Company, LLC
P.O. BOX 6232
Compton, CA 90224
Email: nonattyssarep@gmail.com

In association with:
Elite Online Publishing
63 East 11400 South
Suite #230
Sandy, UT 84070
EliteOnlinePublishing.com

ISBN: 978-1-961801-84-4 (eBook)
ISBN: 978-1-961801-98-1 (Paperback)

POL027000
REF015000

LIBRARY OF CONGRESS CONTROL NUMBER: 2024917113

QUANTITY PURCHASES: Schools, companies, professional groups, clubs, and other organizations may qualify for special terms when ordering quantities of this title.
For information, email nonattyssarep@gmail.com
All rights reserved by JUDITH WHITE-LARKINS.
This book is printed in the United States of America.

DEDICATION
TO MY MOTHER

My book is dedicated to the sweetest and kindest
person, whose nurturing, understanding, and
parental guidance have groomed me
into the person I am today.

The most Dearest and 'Special' I love to call,
"Mother", Mrs. Gracie M. Perry.
Mother, I Love You with all my heart.

TABLE OF CONTENTS

DISABILITY

"An impairment of mind and body
which continuously renders it impossible for
the disabled person to follow any substantial
gainful occupation, and was likely to last for
the rest of a person's life."

Disability Insurance Law–July 1956

FOREWORD

Where it is written you can't get your Social Security Disability Benefits on the first attempt... Judith White-Larkins, a Non-Attorney Social Security Appointed Representative, always wanted to solve the problem of prospective applicants or claimants getting denied repeatedly and not getting approved on their first attempt.

She'd say, "*Americans are experiencing too many social security disability insurance (SSDI) and supplemental security income (SSI) benefit award denials*".

A CBS News Correspondent interviewed Scott Watson, 33 years old, who has failed Surgery, which left Watson with a fracture in his spinal cord. Declared disabled by the State of Maryland, Watson was told he was a "shoo-in." When he applied for Federal disability last year, only to be denied, on the grounds that, according to Federal guidelines, under the Social Security Act, he was not disabled enough. Watson appealed and was denied again. Each year, the Social Security Administration denies almost two-thirds (66 out of 100) of the initial claims it receives. To put it another way, 34 out of 100 clients get approved. If you're reading this, you probably fit into the 66 out of 100. Once you get denied, the requirements seem to multiply. This could lead to a lengthy and complicated appeals process.

The number one cause for Social Security Denials is as follows: your lawyer, your lawyer, and your lawyer... not the Administrative Law Judge (ALJ) at the hearing, who has federal guidelines to follow to prove your case. Scott Watson was denied because the paperwork was not in line with the federal guidelines. In other words, on paper, he wasn't "disabled enough". The ALJ doesn't care how bad your physical condition looks, or how bad you feel, or how you are acting, as a matter of fact, you don't even have to be present at the hearing. You've heard the saying, "Justice is Blind." Well, that may not always be true when it comes to the criminal or civil court proceedings, but at the disability hearing, justice is blind; your paperwork should do your talking for you.

You're an intelligent person, ask yourself this simple question: why does a person with an obvious disability, an amputated leg or arm get denied? Not just once but a second or third time, if it's just about your physical condition... if it's just about your physical or mental condition, you wouldn't need a lawyer, the condition would speak for itself.

You'd just roll, crawl, or limp yourself into the hearing, the Judge would look at you, see an amputated leg or arm, glance at your paperwork, "Oh, you can't drive a bus any longer, claim approved." You're out of there, on your first attempt.

A prospective applicant or claimant pursuing a determination of eligibility for benefits should read this book, because most other books on Disability discuss only Social Security and SSI, without clearing up other vital factors. White-Larkins' tells the reader how to apply for all the programs they should from the outset.

**Do you need representation? Email us at:
nonattyssarep@gmail.com**

CHAPTER 1

STATE DISABILITY INSURANCE

State Disability Insurance is disability (money) that you can receive when you become unable to work in the state in which you reside. You, the employee, pay into state disability insurance while you are working; it comes out of your payroll check each pay period.

STATES THAT HAVE SDI

State Disability Insurance is disability (money) paid to you when you are unable to work, in the following states: (1)

California, (2)Hawaii, (3)Rhode Island, (4)New Jersey, (5) New York and (6)Puerto Rico, have state-mandated short-term disability programs that provide wage replacement to eligible employees

Here's a more detailed breakdown:

States with State-Mandated Short-Term Disability Programs:

o California: Offers State Disability Insurance (SDI) through the Employment Development Department (EDD).

o Hawaii: Provides Temporary Disability Insurance (TDI) through the Disability Compensation Division.

o New Jersey: Has a state-run temporary disability program.

o New York: Offers Short-Term Disability Benefits (DBL).

o Rhode Island: Provides Temporary Disability Insurance (TDI).

o Puerto Rico: Also has a state-mandated short-term disability program.

How these programs are funded: Each state funds its disability program differently, whether it be through employee wage deductions and/or employer contributions.

Private Insurance Options: In some states, employers can offer coverage through a private insurer after receiving approval from the relevant state agency.

SDI vs. Workers' Compensation: State Disability Insurance (SDI) covers non-work-related disabilities, while Workers' Compensation covers injuries or illnesses that occur on the job.

Paid Family and Medical Leave (PFML): Some of the states with SDI also have paid family and medical leave programs.

STATE DISABILITY PROCESS

1. Call your local unemployment office in the state where you reside for a state disability application form.

2. Once you receive the state disability application form, you will receive the attached forms:

   a. Employee Information form

   b. HIPAA State form (see SDI)

   c. Questionnaire, stating whether your disability was job-related or caused by a job injury.

   d. If it is job-related, did you file a Worker's Compensation claim?

   e. A Certificate of Medical Disability is a form that should be filled out by a medical physician stating the appropriate disabling condition.

   f. Once the medical physician fills out the Certificate of Medical Disability, he then mails it back to the office to qualify for the disability.

   g. You will wait for a wage computation from the SDI office, which you will receive in the mail.

SDI WAITING PERIOD

State Disability Waiting Period is usually a 14-day waiting period; you will receive your first weekly benefit after you have been declared disabled by your medical physician.

THE LENGTH OF
STATE DISABILITY INSURANCE

The length of your state disability insurance depends on how the medical physician states the findings of your medical/mental condition, which should give you a reasonable cause to be disabled. The length of your state disability insurance can vary from 1 week (7 days) to 1 year (52 weeks).

REFERRAL FROM
THE STATE DISABILITY PHYSICIAN

Sometimes, if you have been on state disability insurance for more time than is allotted initially with your medical/mental disabling condition, the state panel of physicians will schedule you to see one of their state physicians to see if you are able to return to your work. It is very important that you schedule the appointment, and please be in compliance with the state. If you don't see the state physician or miss your appointment, your SDI benefits will be discontinued. Your benefits will also discontinue while you are waiting to see the state physician.

HOW YOU WILL RECEIVE PAYMENTS FROM STATE DISABILITY INSURANCE VIA THE EDD OFFICE

1. Starting January 15, 2024, EDD disability benefits are now paid to the individual with a Money Network prepaid Debit card from the EDD office.

   (Paper checks are no longer used).

2. Activating your EDD card- there is a toll-free number to activate your card, using the last four digits of your Social Security number or whatever number you prefer to use.

THE APPEAL PROCESS FOR STATE DISABILITY INSURANCE

1. When you have been disqualified from SDI.

2. You should request to file an appeal with the SDI Worker.

3. Ask them to do a "Special Wage Computation".

"SPECIAL WAGE COMPUTATION FOR SDI"

1. What constitutes a "special wage computation"?

   For example, you were receiving Unemployment Insurance Benefits (UIB) for over a period of six months to three years or more. (Those same UIB wages can be used to receive a "special wage computation".

2. When applying for a "special wage computation"

   a. Write a request letter stating that you would like to do a special wage computation from the time you initially stopped working.

   b. There is a form that SDI will send you in the mail.

HOW TO ACQUIRE A SPECIAL WAGE COMPUTATION FOR SDI

When you have been denied for SDI, because no money was in the quarters for the period, for the SDI to pay, since you have not worked, you have received (UIB) unemployment insurance benefits, for a period of six months to three years or more, at this time.

"Please ask the SDI representative to send a special wage compensation form to determine your wages, so that you may become qualified for SDI."

CONDITIONS THAT QUALIFY YOU FOR STATE DISABILITY INSURANCE

1. Medical conditions that will qualify you for state disability insurance are: Hypertension-high blood pressure, Migraine Headaches, Heart conditions—congestive heart failure, arteriosclerotic heart disease, enlarged heart, defective valve, Back problems—lumbar disc disease, low back disease, etc.

2. Mental conditions—that will qualify for state disability insurance are: Post Traumatic Stress Disorder, Depressive Neurosis, Bipolar, Manic Depression, Paranoid Schizophrenia, and Schizo-Affective.

HOW TO RECEIVE STATE DISABILITY INSURANCE (SDI) FREQUENTLY ASKED QUESTIONS (FAQ) WITH ANSWERS

1. What is State Disability Insurance?

   State Disability Insurance is what you (employee) pay out of your paycheck, bi-weekly or monthly.

2. Did you ever apply for SDI and were disqualified?

   If you did, there are other ways to apply for state disability insurance after being disqualified and still receive benefits.

3. What are the requirements for State Disability Insurance?

   a. Have been employed on a taxable income job.

   b. Became ill and unable to work on your job.

   c. Consulted your medical physician about your disabling condition.

   d. Your medical physician declares you are disabled and unable to perform work on your job.

4. How are your benefits paid to you from State Disability Insurance?

   Your benefits from State Disability Insurance are paid on a bi-weekly basis at a rate of 60-70% of your regular wages, for at least 52 weeks.

5. What constitutes that you have been qualified for State Disability Insurance?

When you are declared disabled by your medical physician, your highest quarter determines your weekly benefit and qualifies you for SDI.

CHAPTER 2

SOCIAL SECURITY
DISABILITY INSURANCE—SSDI

Social Security Disability Insurance can only be applied for:

1. When you are unemployed,

2. Has received State Disability Insurance, if living in your state, for at least 52 weeks (which is a year), for a medical or mental condition, in which the individual is not able to work in the workforce indefinitely.

APPLYING FOR SSDI

1. Call the Social Security toll-free number: (800)772-1213 between the hours of 7:00 A.M.-7:00 P.M. PST, EST, MST, and CST.

2. When speaking to a "live" representative, tell them you are totally disabled and would like to apply for Social Security Disability Insurance.

3. The representative will ask you the following information:
   a. Your Social Security Number
   b. Your legal given name
   c. Your Place of Birth
   d. Your mailing address and telephone number
   e. Your date of birth
   f. Your Mother's maiden name

4. Then the representative will repeat the information that you gave, to see if everything is correct.

5. The representative will tell you that an application for SSDI will be mailed within 7-10 days, respectfully.

6. Once you receive the application, you should go to your medical physician to assist you in filling out the medical portion.

   a. The physician will diagnose you, the patient's medical condition.

   b. The physician will order additional medical procedures (blood tests, x-rays, etc.)

7. Also, your work record is a very important factor when applying for SSDI in order to determine your SSDI benefits. Be sure to write your Work history correctly. (Work history from age of eligibility to work until the present).

THE SSDI PROCESS AFTER THE PREPARATION

1. You will receive a Work History Report.

2. You will receive a Daily Questionnaire (These documents will come from Social Security).

WORK HISTORY REPORT

1. Social Security has all of your Work History, from your first job to your last job.

2. The Work history report wants to determine if you have been employed since you applied for SSDI.

3. Did your Job require lifting?

4. If your Job required any lifting, how many pounds did you lift in an 8-hour day?

5. Your Job Title.

6. Description of Job Duties.

AFTER YOU HAVE RECEIVED
THE WORK HISTORY REPORT AND
DAILY QUESTIONNAIRE

1. Contact the SSDI Analyst who is handling your disability claim.

2. Then, get their permission to fax the documents that were mailed to you by the Social Security Administration.

3. If you have any tests, x-rays, documents, including H&P (HISTORY AND PHYSICAL), or any medical records, needed to support your case.

PREPARING YOURSELF FOR A SOCIAL SECURITY DISABILITY EXAM

When you prepare yourself for a Social Security Disability Exam, you should do the following things:

1. Depending on your Medical or Mental condition, please have current tests (x-rays, MRIs, blood tests, or CT Scans).

2. Make sure that you have recent medical records within a six-month period.

3. Get your own copies of Medical Records from the agencies that are performing the procedure, or the needed procedure.

4. Please take the Medical Records to the Disability Exam.

THINGS TO TAKE TO YOUR EXAM
FOR A MEDICAL OR MENTAL CONDITION

1. For a Heart Condition, take your current EKG (Electrocardiogram), your Echocardiogram for a mitral valve prolapse, and all of your prescribed Medications, as well as OTC (over the counter) and current Lab results (blood tests, etc).

2. X-ray of the L/S Spine (Lumbosacral), include your prescribed medications, as well as OTC (over the counter). If you had Physical Therapy, describe: What Type of Physical Therapy? Electrical Stimulation, Hot or Cold packs, Massage, or Diathermy.

3. For a Mental or Psychological disorder, you need to bring all of your Medical records from the Psychiatrist or Psychologist. Bring your prescribed medications. With a Mental disorder.

4. You could be treated for: Severe Depression, Manic Depression, Bi-Polar, Schizophrenia, or Schizo-Affective, Post Traumatic Stress Disorder, or Depressive Neurosis. Please include all Mental Exams (such as mental testing, blood levels of medications, etc).

5. All of your medical records are from your neurologist. Please include test results (CT Scans of the Skull, EEGs, and encephalograms). Be sure to bring your prescribed medications, Such as Dilantin, Depakote, or Phenobarbital, and blood levels of your medications. Please include the frequencies of your Seizure or Epilepsy episodes.

DAILY QUESTIONNAIRE FOR SSDI

The daily questionnaire will ask many questions about your daily activities:

1. Where do you live?

2. With whom do you live?

3. Do you drive a car?

4. How far can you drive?

5. How far can you walk?

6. Do you do grocery shopping?

7. Do you do household chores?

8. What do you do in an 8-hour day?

9. What medications are you taking?

10. What are the dosages of your medications?

11. Can you lift anything?

12. If you can lift, up to how many pounds?

PAIN QUESTIONNAIRE FOR SSDI

The pain questionnaire is a questionnaire that determines the degree of pain in your medical condition. Sent by the Social Security state office.

1. Where is your pain?

2. How long does your pain last?

3. What kind of pain?
   a. Sharp pain
   b. Aching pain
   c. excruciating pain
   d. stabbing pain
   e. throbbing pain

4. Levels of Pain (On a scale of 1-10)
   a. Standing pain
   b. Sitting pain
   c. Lying down pain
   d. Walking pain

5. What time does the pain that you have occur?

    a. Night time

    b. Morning time

    c. All the time

    d. All day long

    e. All night long

6. How do you relieve your pain?

    a. OTC (over-the-counter) medications - found in drug stores or pharmacies.

    b. Prescription medications - written on a prescription by your medical physician.

TYPES OF PAIN

1. Chest pain pertaining to the heart muscle or the digestive tract, such as indigestion, heartburn, dysphagia, etc.

2. Back pain pertaining to the lumbar sacral region of the back.

3. Arthritic joint pain in the knee, shoulder, hip, leg, etc.

4. Migraine headaches - pain in all the lobes of the brain (Temporal, Frontal, Occipital, and Parietal).

5. Injury pain pertaining to sprains and strains of the muscles and tissues.

6. Abdominal pain like (gastric) - duodenum or peptic (ulcer) pancreas and liver.

7. Internal organ pain pertaining to your gallbladder, kidneys, urinary bladder, uterus, prostate gland, along with the rectum and anus.

METHODS OF RELIEVING
YOUR PAIN

1. Pain Medication

2. Physical Therapy - electrical stimulation, hot or cold packs, massage or diathermy

3. Braces

4. Crutches

5. Canes

6. Wheel Chairs

7. Scooters

WHEN GOING TO THE STATE DOCTOR FOR SOCIAL SECURITY DISABILITY

1. Have a current State Driver's License or State Identification card, and correctly identify yourself.

2. Bring a copy of your letter to the appointment to see the state doctor.

3. You will be given an information form to fill out when you arrive there.

4. After you have filled out the form, you will then give it back to the front desk personnel.

5. Then you will wait for your time to be called to be seen by the state doctor.

WHEN TAKING THE SSDI EXAM

1. The physician will only ask you to identify yourself (with a current state identification card or driver's license, which must include a picture).

2. Date of Birth

3. Take your Vital Signs: B/P - Blood Pressure, WT - Weight, HT - Height, T. - Temperature

4. Lastly, ask a series of questions about your medical condition.

5. The physician will ask when you last worked and what type of work you were performing.

6. With your condition, could you work fewer hours, or take a sit-down position?

7. The physician will try to confuse you, that is, even if you are disabled, you can work.

8. No blood work, EKGs, X-rays, or any tests are given during the exam.

WHEN YOU ARE APPROVED
FOR SOCIAL SECURITY DISABILITY

1. You will receive an Award Letter - A letter that grants you approval for Social Security Disability benefits, which will give you your Monthly Benefit amount.

2. You will receive a telephone call from your SSDI Analyst in your local Social Security office to come into the office for an SSDI Approval visit.

3. During the visit, your SSDI Analyst He/She will explain all the information about your SSDI approval.

4. You will be given a period of approximately eight weeks from the SSDI Analyst before you receive your first monthly benefit check.

5. Your SSDI check can be directly deposited to your bank or financial Institution of your choice.

6. Your SSDI check can also be put on a Social Security Debit Card.

MAINTAINING YOUR SSDI AFTER BEING APPROVED

1. Continue to seek medical care from your current physician.

2. Take all of the Procedures that your physician requests (Blood tests, EKGs, X-rays, MRIs, etc).

3. If given medications to take for your medical condition, be sure to comply with your physician's directions.

4. Try to make monthly appointments to get regular check-ups.

5. Always confirm your appointment on the day before your appointment.

6. When you can't make the appointment, call your physician's office to reschedule your appointment.

PLEASE NOTE: TO ALL SSDI BENEFICIARIES

The Social Security Administration could call you in for an evaluation at any time to make sure you are still disabled, under the guidelines of the Social Security Act. You have to be totally available and prepared for your SSDI interview. Sometimes, the interview may be done on a random basis.

HOW TO GET APPROVED FOR SSDI, ONCE YOU'VE BEEN DENIED

1. You have to produce 'new' Medical or Mental Information.

2. All information has to be very current.

3. Call the State Capital in your State for their Social Security office.

   a. Ask the State Social Security office to reopen your SSDI case.

   b. That means to locate the office of Social Security that denied your case.

   c. If the office reopens your case

      i. You will go back to the state physicians

      ii. The Doctors will realize that an error has occurred

      iii. You will be granted approval for SSDI

WHEN YOUR SSDI CLAIM IS DENIED

1. You will receive a Denial letter for SSDI in the mail.

2. You have 60 days to make an appeal.

3. You can request a hearing.

4. You can go to a hearing before an Administrative Law Judge (ALJ).

5. You can do a reconsideration - explain why you disagree with the SSDI denial.

6. Reopen your case by calling your state capital's Social Security office to locate it so that it may be reopened and re-evaluated for errors.

REASON FOR SSDI DENIAL

Under Social Security guidelines, when you are denied, you didn't meet the requirements for a disabled person, according to the Social Security Act.

IF DENIED FOR SSDI

1. Call Social Security's toll-free number: (800) 772-1213, for a reconsideration form.

2. Request a Legal hearing:

   a. Administrative Law Judge hearing

   b. Regular hearing by a State Panel for SSDI.

HEARING TIME LIMIT

If you are going to file a hearing, the hearing must be done within a 60-day period.

HEARING PROCESSING
TIME FOR SSDI

Hearing Processing Time could take approximately from 60 days to 12 months (Depending on the disability claims that are already pending).

The Administrative Law Judge has to look for an open appointment on his/her hearing schedule, for availability on his/her calendar. It could take up to 60 days to 12 months.

FREQUENTLY ASKED
QUESTIONS (FAQS) ABOUT SSDI

1. What is Social Security Disability Insurance?

2. What is totally disabled?

3. What is Work History?

4. When will you receive the SSDI disability application?

5. What is the difference between an office appointment and a telephone appointment?

6. What happens during the 30-90-day period?

7. How does the physician aid the disabled patient?

8. What happened when you were approved for Social Security Disability Insurance?

9. What is an Award Letter?

10. What is Direct Deposit?

11. What are some of the reasons for being denied for Social Security Disability Insurance?

12. What happens during the "hearing" of the denied Social Security Disability Insurance?

13. How do you "Reopen" your denied Social Security Disability Insurance case?

14. What are the different types of appeals for a Social Security Disability Insurance case?

15. What is a "Reconsideration" appeal for a Social Security Disability Insurance denial?

SOCIAL SECURITY DISABILITY INSURANCE GLOSSARY FOR SSDI

Social Security Disability Insurance is when you have worked in the employment market, and have become disabled, and aren't able to work anymore.

Totally disabled is when a person is not able to work, due to a Medical or Mental Condition.

Work history is from the age of eligibility, when you are able to work, at least from 18 years of age, to the present.

Office appointment is when you are scheduled to go to the local Social Security office in your area, where you reside.

Telephone appointments are usually made in your place of residence by a Social Security Representative from your local office, who will call you on the telephone. The times of the appointment may vary from the morning to the evening, whichever you prefer.

The 30-90 day processing of your Social Security SSDI claim will be thoroughly reviewed during that time.

Daily Questionnaire Application is a questionnaire sent to you by the State Department of California.

1. One questionnaire is for you - the applicant;
2. One third-party questionnaire - for someone who knows you very well.

When you are approved for SSDI, you will receive your Benefits for SSDI within 8 weeks from the approval date.

Documents That Are Needed On Approval - Cl) Your Original License or State Identification card.

An Award Letter is a letter from Social Security with the Monthly Benefit amount that you will receive (It will be mailed to you.)

Direct Deposit is a relationship between your bank and Social Security, where you receive an electronic transfer to the bank for your monthly benefits.

Monthly Benefit is the amount of your Social Security benefit each month.

Determination of Disability Benefits - to determine your SSDI benefits, you must have acquired 40 credits during the quarters of your total Work history. (Social Security takes the lowest wages in the first 10 years and deducts them.)

CASE HISTORY OF APPROVED DISABILITY PATIENTS STATE DISABILITY INSURANCE

Name: Patient A Age: 56 Gender: Male

In the year 2018, I went to my local pharmacy, I happened to meet a Woman who I had previously spoken to. She told me, "that she was a Licensed Life Insurance Agent," I told her that I had Life Insurance already. We exchanged Phone numbers. I told her that I was a Non-Attorney Social Security Appointed Representative. Two weeks later, I received a call from her husband, whom I will call Patient A.

He explained to me that he was disabled and was unable to work anymore.

I asked him, how long has he been off work? He told me for about three months or more. He also had received Unemployment Insurance Benefits (UIB). I had explained to him that in order to apply for Disability, in the State of California, He has to file for SDI-State Disability Insurance first for one year, because it's a temporary disability. He had to go to EDD-Employment Development Department to request a printout, due to his exhaustion of his Unemployment Insurance Benefits (UIB).

After that, I told him that I was a Non-Attorney Social Security Appointed Representative and could fill out the SDI application form.

Then I'll take him to my Former employer, a Medical Physician, to see him as a new patient, and put him on SDI.

I had previously worked for the Physician, filling out the Medical portion of SDI forms.

I scheduled an appointment for him to see my Former employer, the Medical Physician.

Patient A was put on SDI for increments of three months, initially, every three months, until it had finally exhausted, in one year's time.

Patient A was diagnosed with the following Medical Conditions:

1. Chronic Cervical Strain

2. Chronic Left Hip Strain

3. Chronic Right Hip Strain

4. Meniscus Tear Right Knee

5. Meniscus Tear Left Knee

CHAPTER 3

SUPPLEMENTAL SECURITY INCOME

SUPPLEMENTAL SECURITY INCOME - is better known as SSI

APPLYING FOR SSI

1. Call the toll-free number: (800) 772-1213 to seek an application for SSI.

2. Ask to speak to a Representative.

3. Questions that the Representative will ask you
   a. Your Social Security Number
   b. Your place of birth
   c. Your legal given name
   d. Your mailing address and telephone number
   e. Your Mother's maiden Name

4. The Representative will mail you an application for SSI - it will take at least 7-10 days.

HOW THE SSI PROCESS WORKS

1. Once you've received your application

   a. You will need to complete your Work history (All work that you have done, from the past to the present).

   b. Complete your medical history; please see if your medical doctor will fill out the medical portion of the SSI application for you.

2. Making an appointment with an SSI Field Representative

   a. You can receive a telephone interview or:

   b. An office appointment interview with the local Social Security office (area that you reside in).

3. Copy of your original birth certificate.

4. Copy of your Social Security card.

THE SSI FIRST PROCESS AFTER THE PREPARATION

1. You will receive a Work History Report.

2. You will receive a Daily Questionnaire. (These documents will come from Social Security).

WORK HISTORY REPORT

1. Social Security has your work history from your first job to your last job.

2. The Work History Report - wants to determine if you have been employed since you applied for SSI.

3. Did your job require any lifting?

4. If your job required any lifting, how many pounds did you lift in an 8-hour day?

5. Your job title.

6. Description of your job duties.

AFTER YOU HAVE RECEIVED THE WORK HISTORY REPORT AND DAILY QUESTIONNAIRE

1. Contact the SSI Analyst who is handling your disability claim.

2. Then get their permission to fax your documents that were mailed to you by the Social Security Administration.

3. If you have any tests, X-rays, or MRI, please attach all documents, including an H&P (HISTORY AND PHYSICAL), or any medical records, needed to support your case.

PREPARE YOURSELF FOR
AN SSI DISABILITY EXAM

When you prepare yourself for an SSI Disability Exam, you should do the following things:

1. Depending on your Medical or Mental Condition, please have current tests: (X-rays, MRIs, Blood tests, or CT Scans).

2. Make sure you have recent medical records within a six-month period.

3. Get your copies of Medical records from the Agencies that are performing the procedures or the needed procedure.

4. Please take the Medical records to the Disability Exam.

THINGS TO TAKE TO YOUR SSI EXAM FOR A MEDICAL OR MENTAL

1. For a Heart Condition, take your current EKG (electrocardiogram for a Mitral Valve Prolapse, and all of your prescribed medications, as well as OTC (over the counter) and current Lab results (Blood tests, etc).

2. For a Back Condition, take your current MRIs, CT Scans, or X-ray of the L/S Spine (Lumbosacral). Include your prescribed medications, as well as OTC (over the counter). If you had Physical Therapy, describe: What type of Physical Therapy? Electrical Stimulation, Hot or Cold packs, Massage, or Diathermy.

3. For a Mental or Psychological Disorder, you need to take all of your Medical records from your Psychiatrist or Psychologist. Take your prescribed medications. With a Mental Disorder, you could be treated for: Severe Depression, Manic Depression, Bipolar, Schizophrenia, or Schizo-Affective, Post Traumatic Stress Disorder, or Depressive Neurosis. Please include all Mental Exams (such as Mental tests, Blood levels of medications, etc).

4. For a Seizure or Epilepsy Disorder, please take all of your Medical records from your Neurologist. Please include test results (CT Scans of the Skull), EEGs, Dilantin, Depakote, or Phenobarbitol levels. Please include the frequencies of your Seizure or Epilepsy episodes.

DAILY QUESTIONNAIRE FOR SSI

The daily questionnaire will ask many questions about your daily activities:

1. Where do you live?

2. With whom do you live?

3. Do you drive a car?

4. How far can you drive?

5. How far can you walk?

6. Do you do grocery shopping?

7. Do you do household chores?

8. What do you do in an 8-hour day?

9. What medications are you taking?

10. What are the dosages of your medications?

11. Can you lift anything?

12. If you can lift, up to how many pounds?

PAIN QUESTIONNAIRE FOR SSI

The Pain Questionnaire is a questionnaire that determines the degree of pain in your medical condition. It is sent by the State Office for Social Security.

1. Where is your pain?

2. How long does your pain last?

3. What kind of pain?
   a. Sharp pain
   b. Aching pain
   c. excruciating pain
   d. stabbing pain
   e. throbbing pain

4. Levels of Pain (On a scale of 1-10)
   a. Standing pain
   b. Sitting pain
   c. Lying down pain
   d. Walking pain

5. What time does the pain that you have occur?
   a. Night time
   b. Morning time

   c. All the time

   d. All day long

   e. All night long

6. How do you relieve your pain?

   a. OTC (over-the-counter medications) - found in Drugstores or pharmacies.

   b. Prescription medications - written by your medical physician.

TYPES OF PAIN

1. **Chest pain** pertaining to the heart muscle or the digestive tract, such as indigestion, heartburn, dysphagia, etc.

2. **Back pain** pertaining to the lumbar sacral region of the back.

3. **Arthritic joint pain** in the knee, shoulder, hip, leg, etc.

4. **Migraine headaches** - pain in all the lobes of the brain (temporal, frontal, occipital, and parietal).

5. **Injury pain** pertaining to sprains and strains of the muscles and tissues.

6. **Abdominal pain** pertaining to the stomach (gastric), duodenum, or peptic (ulcer) pancreas and liver.

7. **Internal Organ pain** pertaining to gallbladder, kidney, bladder, uterus, prostate, rectum and anus.

METHODS OF RELIEVING PAIN

1. Pain medication

2. Physical Therapy - electrical stimulation, hot or cold packs, massage, or diathermy.

3. Braces

4. Crutches

5. Canes

6. Wheel Chairs

7. Scooters

WHEN GOING TO THE
STATE DOCTOR FOR SSI DISABILITY

1. Have a Current State Driver's License or Identification Card to correctly identify yourself.

2. Bring a copy of your letter to the appointment to see the state doctor.

3. You will be given an Information form when you arrive there.

4. After you have filled the form out, you will then give it back to the front desk personnel.

5. Then you will wait for the time to be called to be seen by the state doctor.

WHEN TAKING THE SSI EXAM

1. The physician will ask you to identify yourself (with a Current State Identification Card, or a Driver's License which must include a picture).

2. Your Date of Birth.

3. Take your Vital Signs: B/P-Blood Pressure, WT.

4. Weight, HT.-Height, T-Temperature.

5. Lastly, the physician will ask a series of questions about your medical condition.

6. The physician will ask when you last worked and what type of work you were performing.

7. With your medical condition, could you work fewer hours, or take a sit-down position?

8. The physician will try to confuse you, that is, even if you are disabled, you can work.

9. No blood work, EKGs, X-rays, or any other tests are given during the exam.

WHEN YOU ARE APPROVED
FOR SSI DISABILITY

1. You will receive an Award Letter - a letter that grants you approval for SSI benefits, which will give you your Monthly Benefit amount.

2. You will receive a telephone call from your SSI Analyst in your local Social Security office to come into the office for an SSI approval visit.

3. During the visit with your SSI Analyst, He/She will explain all the information about your SSI Disability approval.

4. You will be given a period of approximately eight weeks from the SSI Analyst before you receive your first Monthly Benefit check.

5. Your SSI Disability check can be directly deposited to your bank or financial Institution of your choice.

6. Your SSI Disability check can also be put on a Social Security Debit Card.

MAINTAINING YOUR SSI BENEFITS AFTER BEING APPROVED

1. Continue to seek medical care from your current physician.

2. Take all of the Procedures that your physician requests (Blood tests, EKGs, X-rays, MRIs, etc).

3. If given medications to take for your medical condition, be sure to comply with your Physician's directions.

4. Try to make monthly appointments to get regular check-ups.

5. Always confirm your appointment on the day before your appointment.

6. When you can't make the appointment, call your Physician's office to reschedule your appointment.

WHEN YOUR SSI IS DENIED

1. You will receive a Denial letter for SSI in the mail.

2. You have 60 days to make an appeal.

3. You can request a hearing.

4. You can go to a hearing before an Administrative Law Judge (ALJ).

5. You can do a reconsideration by explaining why you disagree with the SSI denial.

6. Reopen your case by calling your State capital's Social Security office to locate your case, so that it may be reopened and re-evaluated for errors.

REASON FOR SSI DENIAL

Under the Social Security guide, when you are denied, you didn't meet the requirements for a disabled person, according to the Social Security Act.

IF DENIED FOR SSI

1. Call Social Security's toll-free number: (800)772-1213, for the Reconsideration form.

2. Request a Legal hearing:

3. Administrative Law Judge hearing
   a. Regular hearing before a state panel, for SSI

HEARING TIME LIMIT

If you are going to file a hearing, the hearing must be done within a 60-day period.

HEARING PROCESSING TIME
FOR SSI

Hearing Process Time - could take approximately 60 days to 12 months. (Depending on the disability claims that are already pending.)

The Administrative Law Judge has to look for an appointment on his/her calendar. It could take from 60 days to 12 months.

HOW TO GET APPROVED FOR SSI, ONCE YOU'VE BEEN DENIED

1. You have to produce 'new' Medical or Mental Information.

2. All information has to be very current.

3. Call the State Capital in your State for their Social Security office. (Ask the State Social Security office to reopen your SSI case.)

   a. That means to locate the office of Social Security that denied your case.

   b. If the office re-opens your case

      i. You will go back to the State Physicians

      ii. You will be re-evaluated

      iii. The doctors will realize an error has occurred

      iv. You will then be granted approval for SSI

SUPPLEMENTAL SECURITY INCOME INSURANCE GLOSSARY FOR SSI

Supplemental Security Income Insurance is when you have become disabled and aren't able to work anymore.

Totally disabled is when a person is not able to work, due to a Medical or Mental condition.

Work History is from the age of eligibility, when you are able to work, at least 18 years of age, to the present.

Office appointment is when you are scheduled to go to the local Social Security office in your area, where you reside.

Telephone appointment is usually done in your place of residence, by a Social Security Representative, from your local office, who calls you on the telephone. The times of the appointment may vary from the morning to the evening, whichever you prefer.

The 30-90 day processing of your Supplemental Security Income Insurance application is the processing period for SSI. The claim will be thoroughly reviewed during that time.

Daily Questionnaire Application - a questionnaire will be sent to you by the State Department of California. (1) One questionnaire is for you, the applicant; (2) One third-party party for someone who knows you very well.

When you are approved for SSI, you will receive your benefits for SSI within 8 weeks from the approval date.

Documents that are needed for approval will need

1. Your Original Birth Certificate

2. Current State Driver's License or State Identification card.

An Award Letter is a letter from Social Security with the Monthly Benefit amount that you will receive. It will be mailed to you.

Direct Deposit is a relationship between your Bank and Social Security, for you to receive an electronic transfer to the Bank for your Monthly Benefits.

Monthly Benefit - the amount of your SSI Benefit each month.

Determination of Disability Benefits - To determine your SSI Benefits, you didn't meet the 40 credits that were required by the Social Security Act in the quarters of your Work history.

CASE STUDIES

CASE HISTORY OF APPROVED DISABILITY PATIENTS SOCIAL SECURITY DISABILITY INSURANCE

Name: Patient A Age:56 Gender: Male

Then in 2019, Patient A applied for SSDI-Social Security Disability Insurance.

My Former employer-A Medical Physician-allowed me to fill out Patient A's medical forms.

At the same time, I was able to fill out an Appointed Representative Form-SSA 1696. Patient A asked me to be his Appointed Representative for Social Security Disability.

Patient A's Medical Physician requested the following:

MRI'S

1. Cervical Spine

2. Left Hip

3. Right Hip

4. Right Knee

5. Left Knee

In approximately three months, Social Security-Dept of Health Services, Requested the Following Forms:

1. Work History Form

2. Medical History Form With Medications

3. Daily Questionnaire

4. Pain Questionnaire

About three more months, Patient A was scheduled, to go to a State Doctor, for his Disability Evaluation.

When going to the State Doctor, I had instructed Patient A, what items. He should take to see the State Doctor:

1. Current Driver's License or State Identification Card

2. Real ID Card

3. Appointment Letter

4. Your Social Security Card

Following the State Doctor's Appointment, within 60 days, Patient A was Awarded his Social Security Disability Insurance-SSDI BENEFITS. Patient A was approved for SSDI, the very first time.

CASE HISTORY OF APPROVED DISABILITY PATIENTS SUPPLEMENTAL SECURITY INCOME

NAME: Patient B Age: 22 Gender: Male

In the year 2021, I was recommended by a friend, to try to assist her sister, in getting her stepson on SSI. He lived with his stepmom and father.

My Client, I will call him, Patient B. He has been diagnosed with 317-Mild Intellectual disability, F330-MDD-Major Depressive Disorder.

Patient B is the product of a drug-induced Mother. He has a great intellectual Disability, and he has been very withdrawn.

His Mother passed away, when he was a young child.

Patient B stays in his room, most of the time, and he is very depressed and withdrawn.

Patient B cries very often, when thinking about his deceased Mother. He also lost a Brother, at least two years ago.

Patient B communicates only with his Stepmother, rarely with his Father, or his other Siblings.

Patient B is a very depressed young man, and he doesn't eat as healthy as he should.

Patient B had been denied for SSI two times, prior to my taking over his case.

When I took over Patient B's case, I filled out an SSA-1696-Appointment of Representative Form.

Then I started going to the Local Mental Health Center, with Patient B and his Stepmother.

On the first visit, at the Mental Health Center, Patient B was evaluated by a Licensed Clinical Social Worker.

After three months, Patient B was assigned to a Licensed Clinical Psychiatrist.

So, Patient B began having weekly and monthly visits with the both of them.

Under the Social Security Administration Act, when you are denied, more than once, you may qualify to go before a hearing, with an Administrative Law Judge.

Patient B fit the criteria for an Administrative Law Judge hearing.

I filled out the forms with the Office Of Hearing Oerations, for Patient B, To request an Administrative Law Judge Hearing.

My request for the Hearing was granted for Patient B.

On November 16, 2022, was granted an ALJ Hearing.

I had appeared before an Administrative Law Judge, with my Client, Patient B,

In the Judge's chambers, along with his Stepmother.

On arriving at the ALJ hearing, for Patient B, I had all of the Medical records and other documents, to support Patient B's case, I hand presented them to the Judge.

Current Medical Evidence-including an H&P-History and Physical, gets the clients approved each time.

On January 7, 2023, a Notice of Decision was mailed to me-Fully Favorable.

Patient B was officially approved for his SSI.

CASE HISTORY OF APPROVED DISABILITY PATIENTS SOCIAL SECURITY DISABILITY INSURANCE

NAME: Patient C Age: 60 Gender: Male

In the year 2023, I was recommended by my Former Employer-A Medical Physician, to try to help this person, Patient C obtain his Social Security Disability Insurance, because Patient C has been denied twice.

When you've been denied, more than once, The Social Security Act, states that you may qualify for a hearing, before an Administrative Law Judge.

I became Patient's C's Appointed Representative in June 2023. I filled out a SSA -1696 Form-Claimant's Appointment of Representative Form.

Patient C was injured on his Job, in October 2020. He was put on Workers' Compensation, for a period of two years. He had injured his Cervical Spine.

In 2021, He received Surgery on his C/S Spine.

Patient C's Pre-Operative Diagnoses:

1. Cervical Stenosis W/Myeloradiculopathy C-4-5, C-6-7
2. C-5-6 Auto fusion

Post-Operative Diagnoses:

1. Cervical Stenosis W/Myeloradiculopathy
2. C-5-6 Auto fusion

Patient C had the following operation performed:

1. Anterior cervical diskectomy and fusion C-4-5

2. Anterior cervical diskectomy and fusion C-6-7

3. Placement of Structural Interbody device C-4-5

4. Placement of Structural Interbody device C-6-7

5. Placement of Anterior Cervical Plate/Instrumentation C4-7

6. Use of Structural Allograft bone

7. Use of Intraoperative Microscope.

Patient C was given a local Anesthetic.

In October 2023, I contacted the Office of

Hearings Operations in Los Angeles, CA.

To inquire about Patient C's case. He needed to have an Informal Hearing, without an Administrative Law Judge.

Patient C hand carried his Medical Records, to the Office of Hearings Operations.

His Medical Records were presented to the Hearing Officers. They thoroughly examined, Patient C's Medical Evidence.

He was officially approved for his Social Security Disability Insurance on November 15, 2023.

Patient C didn't have to appear, before an Administrative Law Judge.

CASE HISTORY OF APPROVED DISABILITY PATIENTS SUPPLEMENTAL SECURITY INCOME

NAME: Patient D Age: 53 Gender: Female

In November 2023, I had acquired a Prospective Client, who was a relative of a former Client of mine. This person, I will call her Patient D. She was injured on her Job in 2016. At that time, Patient D was put on Workers' Compensation for a period of two years. Her Workers' Compensation Physician declared her totally disabled and unable to work. She applied for SSDI in 2018, following the exhaustion of her Workers' Compensation Benefits. In 2018, Patient D hired a Law Firm, with Multiple Lawyers, to help assist her in obtaining her SSDI benefits. Patient D was not informed of SDI-State Disability Insurance. When she finally found about SDI, the statute of limitations, was only within two years to apply. When applying for SSDI, Patient D also applied for SSI.

The injuries that Patient D received on her Job are the following:

1. Carpal Tunnel Rt. Hand

2. Sprain Rt. Hand

3. Rt. Tennis Elbow, Forearm

4. Severe Anxiety Depression

5. Severe Bouts of Insomnia

6. Severe Fatigue

In 2019, Patient D was first denied by the Social Security Administration. In 2020, Patient D was denied the second time. Finally in 2023, Patient D again was denied the third time with the same Law Firm. The Law Firm advised her, to file a Lawsuit against Social Security.

I had advised my Prospective Client, Patient D, we need to file a new SSDI application with an SSI application, also. Then she had advised me, that she wanted me to represent her. So, I filled out a SSA-1696 Form for Patient D, in order for me to represent her SSDI and SSI disability case. It's called the Appointment of Representative Form. My Client, Patient D suffers with Severe Anxiety Depression. So, I assisted her in finding a Psychiatric Social Worker, along with a Licensed Clinical Psychiatrist. She still sees both of them, at least twice a month.

In November 2024, Patient D was found disabled under SSA guidelines. Patient D was approved for SSI. She had been denied for three times, before I took on her case. She didn't qualify for SSDI, because she didn't have current Medical Records.

But I filed a Reconsideration Form for Patient D with "new" Medical Records, Her SSDI case is currently pending.

CASE HISTORY OF APPROVED
DISABILITY PATIENTS
SOCIAL SECURITY DISABILITY INSURANCE

NAME: PATIENT E AGE: 48 GENDER: FEMALE

In October 1990, I assisted a prospective client in applying for her SSDI. I will call her Patient E. She was a patient in the Physician's Medical Office, where I was employed as a Front Office Medical Assistant. My duties as a Front Office M.A. were to take care of the Insurance Forms, e.g., SDI, SSI, and SSDI, for my employer.

Patient E was having constant pain in her lower back-L/S Spine, and her C/S Spine (neck area). Patient E was being prescribed pain medications by her Physician, but nothing seemed to ease her pain.

Patient E was referred to an Orthopedic Specialist for her Lower Back and Constant Neck pain.

My employer decided to put her on SSDI. Her Orthopedic Specialist recommended that Patient E take the following MRIs: AP-LAT-L/S Spine, and a CT Scan of her back. She was having severe neck pain, She was given an MRI and CT Scan for her Neck-C/S Spine-AP-LAT.

I filled out Patient E's paperwork for SSDI She kept going to the Orthopedic Specialist.

When Patient E was scheduled to see the State Doctor for SSA, Her Medical Evaluation for SSDI was at least six months or more. Her Orthopedic Specialist requested more MRIs and CT Scans for her L/S Spine (Back) and C/S Spine (Neck) for Patient E.

The State Doctors for SSA evaluated Patient E she was found to be disabled by the SSA guidelines. Patient E was approved for SSDI in June 1991.

CASE HISTORY OF APPROVED DISABILITY PATIENTS SOCIAL SECURITY DISABILITY INSURANCE

NAME: PATIENT F AGE: 41 GENDER: Male

In the year 1997, I met a person, who I'd like to call Patient F. When I met him, he told me, "he had a Heart Condition- Congestive Heart Failure, along with Malignant Hypertension.

Patient F was my high school classmate, younger brother. So Patient F and I became friends, so he applied for his SSDI, and asked me to assist him in filling out his SSDI disability forms.

When Patient F turned in his disability forms to SSA, in about three months, Patient F was scheduled to see the State Doctor. I requested that Patient F go to consult with my Cardiologist.

Patient F was prescribed his Cardiac medications by the Cardiologist.

Patient F was found to be disabled. Under the SSA guidelines, He was approved for SSDI in June 1998.

CHAPTER 4

MISCELLANEOUS DISABILITY INFORMATION

MEDICAL INSURANCE COVERAGE FOR SOCIAL SECURITY DISABILITY

After you've been approved for Social Security Disability, you will receive Medicaid or an HMO. When you are disabled for two years. You will receive Medicare, which has two parts: A and B. Part A is for Hospital Insurance, and Part B is for Medical, such as office visits. Then you should be enrolled in Medicare Part D Prescription Drug Coverage.

Medicare is a Federal government program, for which the Monthly premium is $185.00. When you receive Social Security Disability, the state has a program called QMB, which is a state buy-in. It pays both your Federal and State Medical Insurance, as long as you are disabled. If your SSDI Monthly Benefit amount should increase while you are on SSDI, you will have to have your Medicare premiums automatically deducted from your Monthly SSDI Benefits.

Once you have reached the age of Retirement, age 67, your Medical Insurance - Medicare will be automatically deducted from your Social Security Monthly Benefits.

MEDICAL INSURANCE COVERAGE FOR SSI DISABILITY

After you have been approved for SSI Disability, you will receive Medicaid or an HMO, which is paid by the state in which you live. But most of the time, you will receive HMO medical coverage. When you reach the age of retirement, which is 67 years of age, you will be given Medicare Part B which is Medical coverage (office, home, etc.) paid by the state.

Part A Medicare, which is Hospital Insurance, is not covered for SSI Disability.

Most SSI Disability persons are forced to get enrolled in an HMO, because their hospital privileges are not covered. They also need to enroll in a Prescription Drug Plan, Medicare Part D.

When you are enrolled in an HMO, which means Health Maintenance Organization. Under the HMO, there are no emergencies; you have to get Authorization to receive all medical care with an HMO.

All Authorizations are in a certain network of Medical Personnel, Doctors, Dentists, and Pharmacies contracted with the HMO Health Plan.

WHEN YOU DON'T QUALIFY
FOR SSDI, BUT DO QUALIFY FOR SSI

1. Your local Social Security office will send you a Denial letter for SSDI.

2. Afterwards, you will then receive an approval letter for SSI from your local Social Security office.

    a. The Social Security office will then schedule you for your approval appointment.

    b. At that time, the Social Security office explains the reasons for your SSDI denial.

3. The Representative will tell you that under the Social Security Act, a person needs to have 40 credits to be declared disabled; for SSDI, you don't have 40 credits.

4. But you were found to be disabled by the Social Security state doctors; you can only qualify for SSI.

5. At the closing of your SSI interview, you are told when you should expect to receive your first Monthly SSI Benefit check.

6. If you qualify for SSI back pay, you will receive it, following your SSI benefit check.

HEALTH MAINTENANCE ORGANIZATIONS

Health Maintenance Organizations (HMOs) are usually Independent Contractors for the State and can be one of the Medicare managed. When you're considered disabled with Social Security, you need to keep Medicare- Your Primary Insurance coverage.

Because you have the freedom to see any physician without authorization approval, sometimes you may have Medicare as primary coverage and an HMO state-funded coverage as secondary medical coverage.

HOW TO ACQUIRE OR GET YOUR MEDICAL HISTORY RECORDS

1. Go to the Medical or Mental facility where you were treated.

2. Request a Medical Release of Information form. (You will need a copy of the Medical Release form to get your Medical History Records).

3. Then you must fill out the Medical Release Form. (Check all the Information that you need: X-rays, Blood tests, etc).

4. Then sign and date the Medical Release of Information form.

5. Then you will take it to the Medical Records or Health Information Systems department at the facilities where you have received your treatments.

ACQUIRING LAWYERS AND OTHER LEGAL RESOURCES: ONCE DENIED FOR SOCIAL SECURITY OR SSI DISABILITY

1. You have become unemployed and unable to work.

2. Your living conditions may have changed to becoming a "homeless" individual.

3. You have no source of Income, due to your disabling condition.

4. You can't afford to pay: 25% of your Benefits (You are approved for Social Security Disability or SSI Disability).

5. You will need all of your money, including any Back Pay, along with your Monthly Benefit Award.

PLEASE REMEMBER THIS PERTINENT RULE ABOUT LAWYERS OR LEGAL PERSONNEL:

Lawyers or Legal Personnel only give Legal advice. They are not trained Medical Professionals. They only know the Court proceedings, not the end result of your Medical Disability or SSI. In essence, you will have to: Get your Medical Records, Your Denial Letter - if you were denied, acquire new Medical Evidence, to support your case yourself, new tests and Procedures (Blood work, MRIs, X-rays, etc.) These are the things that you have to provide to the Lawyers or Legal Professionals before they can represent you.

FINDING A LAWYER

"INFORMATION ON HOW TO TALK TO A LAWYER, TELL YOUR STORY, AND THE IMPORTANCE OF GATHERING THE FACTS IN YOUR CASE".

QUESTIONS TO ASK A LAWYER, WHEN HIRING ONE

1. What conditions automatically disqualify you for SSDI/SSI?

2. What mistakes or omissions could hurt my chances of getting approved the first time?

3. How will you prepare me for a hearing to testify before an Administrative Law Judge?

4. How long has he/she been a practicing lawyer or a disability advocate?

5. How many cases do you get approved monthly?

6. What do your prospective clients require you to have to represent their disability case?

7. What is your standard fee with a lien after you decide to represent your prospective clients?

8. What documents should the prospective clients present to you before you represent your prospective clients?

9. How can you ensure the prospective clients that if you represent them, you'll get them approved?

10. What do you recommend to a first-time disability prospective client when you decide to represent them?

11. What is needed to represent your prospective client who has been denied one, maybe two, times or more?

12. When agreeing to represent your prospective client, do you: ask for their primary care physicians' medical information, and services that were rendered to the prospective client?

13. When talking to your prospective client, do you ask them when they first became disabled?

14. When were the times your prospective client had been denied? Was it one time, two times, or more times?

15. When overlooking all the information of your prospective clients for you to represent them can you guarantee to them that you'll get them approved?

HOW TO APPLY FOR DISABILITY (SDI, SSDI, SSI) WHEN YOU DON'T HAVE MEDICAL COVERAGE (IF YOU'RE LIVING IN THE STATE OF CALIFORNIA)

If you are Unemployed or a Homeless Individual:

1. Go to the County Welfare office in the area where you live and apply for General Relief (GR).

2. Apply for Medi-Cal Insurance.

3. The application processing time could take from 2 to 6 weeks.

4. Once you've been approved, you will be assigned a Medi-Cal HMO physician.

5. Then you'll be able to apply for Disability (SDI, SSDI, SSI), whichever one you may qualify for.

ABOUT THE AUTHORS

JUDITH WHITE-LARKINS

Non-Attorney Social Security Appointed Representative

Judith White-Larkins is deeply committed to helping individuals navigate the complexities of the Social Security disability system. Drawing from her personal journey navigating the complexities of disability benefits, Judith is dedicated to helping others successfully apply for and secure the assistance they deserve.

After being diagnosed with Congestive Heart Failure and Chronic Angina, she became unable to work and experienced firsthand the challenges of applying for disability benefits. Despite multiple denials, she persisted and ultimately secured Social Security Disability Insurance (SSDI). This difficult process gave her invaluable insight into the system and fueled her passion for assisting others in similar situations.

With over 40 years of experience working alongside physicians to help patients obtain disability benefits, Judith has developed a deep understanding of Social Security Administration guidelines. She later obtained her Non-Attorney Social Security Appointed Representative ID, allowing her to represent disability claimants. She has since successfully represented claimants before the Office of Hearing Operations, helping them secure much-needed benefits.

Judith's mission is to empower individuals struggling with disability claims, particularly those who are homeless or facing repeated denials. Through her book and advocacy work, she provides crucial guidance to help people navigate the complex disability system and receive the support they need.

Do you need representation?
Email us at: nonattyssarep@gmail.com

MICHAEL D. MOORE
Disability Advisor

Michael D. Moore is a retired Radiologic Technologist and co-author of The Complete Guide to Social Security Disability: How to Qualify, Apply, and Maximize Your SSI, SSDI, and State Benefits. Drawing from decades of medical experience and his own journey through work-related injury, Michael brings a unique and compassionate perspective to the complex world of disability benefits.

Now an avid reader, expert chess player, and daily journal writer, Michael joined forces with Non-Attorney Social Security Appointed Representative Judith White-Larkins to create a practical guide that helps individuals get approved the first time. His mission is to provide real answers and real help to those facing life-changing circumstances.

Do you need representation?
Email us at: nonattyssarep@gmail.com

TO DO LIST

MONTH ------------------------------------   DATE ------------------------------------

TO DO

- [ ] ------------------------------------
- [ ] ------------------------------------
- [ ] ------------------------------------
- [ ] ------------------------------------
- [ ] ------------------------------------
- [ ] ------------------------------------
- [ ] ------------------------------------
- [ ] ------------------------------------
- [ ] ------------------------------------
- [ ] ------------------------------------
- [ ] ------------------------------------
- [ ] ------------------------------------
- [ ] ------------------------------------
- [ ] ------------------------------------
- [ ] ------------------------------------
- [ ] ------------------------------------
- [ ] ------------------------------------
- [ ] ------------------------------------
- [ ] ------------------------------------
- [ ] ------------------------------------
- [ ] ------------------------------------
- [ ] ------------------------------------
- [ ] ------------------------------------
- [ ] ------------------------------------
- [ ] ------------------------------------
- [ ] ------------------------------------
- [ ] ------------------------------------
- [ ] ------------------------------------

PRIORITIES

- [ ] ------------------------------------
- [ ] ------------------------------------
- [ ] ------------------------------------
- [ ] ------------------------------------
- [ ] ------------------------------------
- [ ] ------------------------------------
- [ ] ------------------------------------

NOTES

REMINDER

TO DO LIST

MONTH ------------------------------   **DATE** ------------------------------

TO DO

- ☐ ------------------------------
- ☐ ------------------------------
- ☐ ------------------------------
- ☐ ------------------------------
- ☐ ------------------------------
- ☐ ------------------------------
- ☐ ------------------------------
- ☐ ------------------------------
- ☐ ------------------------------
- ☐ ------------------------------
- ☐ ------------------------------
- ☐ ------------------------------
- ☐ ------------------------------
- ☐ ------------------------------
- ☐ ------------------------------
- ☐ ------------------------------
- ☐ ------------------------------
- ☐ ------------------------------
- ☐ ------------------------------
- ☐ ------------------------------
- ☐ ------------------------------
- ☐ ------------------------------
- ☐ ------------------------------
- ☐ ------------------------------
- ☐ ------------------------------
- ☐ ------------------------------
- ☐ ------------------------------

PRIORITIES

- ☐ ------------------------------
- ☐ ------------------------------
- ☐ ------------------------------
- ☐ ------------------------------
- ☐ ------------------------------
- ☐ ------------------------------
- ☐ ------------------------------

NOTES

REMINDER

TO DO LIST

MONTH -------------------------------   **DATE** -------------------------------

TO DO

- ☐ -------------------------------
- ☐ -------------------------------
- ☐ -------------------------------
- ☐ -------------------------------
- ☐ -------------------------------
- ☐ -------------------------------
- ☐ -------------------------------
- ☐ -------------------------------
- ☐ -------------------------------
- ☐ -------------------------------
- ☐ -------------------------------
- ☐ -------------------------------
- ☐ -------------------------------
- ☐ -------------------------------
- ☐ -------------------------------
- ☐ -------------------------------
- ☐ -------------------------------
- ☐ -------------------------------
- ☐ -------------------------------
- ☐ -------------------------------
- ☐ -------------------------------
- ☐ -------------------------------
- ☐ -------------------------------
- ☐ -------------------------------
- ☐ -------------------------------
- ☐ -------------------------------

PRIORITIES

- ☐ -------------------------------
- ☐ -------------------------------
- ☐ -------------------------------
- ☐ -------------------------------
- ☐ -------------------------------
- ☐ -------------------------------
- ☐ -------------------------------

NOTES

REMINDER

TO DO LIST

MONTH -------------------------------   **DATE** -------------------------------

TO DO

- ☐ -------------------------------
- ☐ -------------------------------
- ☐ -------------------------------
- ☐ -------------------------------
- ☐ -------------------------------
- ☐ -------------------------------
- ☐ -------------------------------
- ☐ -------------------------------
- ☐ -------------------------------
- ☐ -------------------------------
- ☐ -------------------------------
- ☐ -------------------------------
- ☐ -------------------------------
- ☐ -------------------------------
- ☐ -------------------------------
- ☐ -------------------------------
- ☐ -------------------------------
- ☐ -------------------------------
- ☐ -------------------------------
- ☐ -------------------------------
- ☐ -------------------------------
- ☐ -------------------------------
- ☐ -------------------------------
- ☐ -------------------------------
- ☐ -------------------------------

PRIORITIES

- ☐ -------------------------------
- ☐ -------------------------------
- ☐ -------------------------------
- ☐ -------------------------------
- ☐ -------------------------------
- ☐ -------------------------------
- ☐ -------------------------------

NOTES

REMINDER

TO DO LIST

MONTH ----------------------------------- **DATE** -----------------------------------

TO DO

☐ -----------------------------------
☐ -----------------------------------
☐ -----------------------------------
☐ -----------------------------------
☐ -----------------------------------
☐ -----------------------------------
☐ -----------------------------------
☐ -----------------------------------
☐ -----------------------------------
☐ -----------------------------------
☐ -----------------------------------
☐ -----------------------------------
☐ -----------------------------------
☐ -----------------------------------
☐ -----------------------------------
☐ -----------------------------------
☐ -----------------------------------
☐ -----------------------------------
☐ -----------------------------------
☐ -----------------------------------
☐ -----------------------------------
☐ -----------------------------------
☐ -----------------------------------
☐ -----------------------------------
☐ -----------------------------------
☐ -----------------------------------
☐ -----------------------------------

PRIORITIES

☐ -----------------------------------
☐ -----------------------------------
☐ -----------------------------------
☐ -----------------------------------
☐ -----------------------------------
☐ -----------------------------------
☐ -----------------------------------

NOTES

REMINDER

TO DO LIST

MONTH -----------------------------------   **DATE** -----------------------------------

TO DO

☐ -----------------------------------
☐ -----------------------------------
☐ -----------------------------------
☐ -----------------------------------
☐ -----------------------------------
☐ -----------------------------------
☐ -----------------------------------
☐ -----------------------------------
☐ -----------------------------------
☐ -----------------------------------
☐ -----------------------------------
☐ -----------------------------------
☐ -----------------------------------
☐ -----------------------------------
☐ -----------------------------------
☐ -----------------------------------
☐ -----------------------------------
☐ -----------------------------------
☐ -----------------------------------
☐ -----------------------------------
☐ -----------------------------------
☐ -----------------------------------
☐ -----------------------------------
☐ -----------------------------------
☐ -----------------------------------
☐ -----------------------------------
☐ -----------------------------------

PRIORITIES

☐ -----------------------------------
☐ -----------------------------------
☐ -----------------------------------
☐ -----------------------------------
☐ -----------------------------------
☐ -----------------------------------
☐ -----------------------------------

NOTES

REMINDER

TO DO LIST

MONTH ---------------------------------- DATE ----------------------------------

TO DO

- ☐ ----------------------------------
- ☐ ----------------------------------
- ☐ ----------------------------------
- ☐ ----------------------------------
- ☐ ----------------------------------
- ☐ ----------------------------------
- ☐ ----------------------------------
- ☐ ----------------------------------
- ☐ ----------------------------------
- ☐ ----------------------------------
- ☐ ----------------------------------
- ☐ ----------------------------------
- ☐ ----------------------------------
- ☐ ----------------------------------
- ☐ ----------------------------------
- ☐ ----------------------------------
- ☐ ----------------------------------
- ☐ ----------------------------------
- ☐ ----------------------------------
- ☐ ----------------------------------
- ☐ ----------------------------------
- ☐ ----------------------------------
- ☐ ----------------------------------
- ☐ ----------------------------------
- ☐ ----------------------------------
- ☐ ----------------------------------
- ☐ ----------------------------------
- ☐ ----------------------------------
- ☐ ----------------------------------

PRIORITIES

- ☐ ----------------------------------
- ☐ ----------------------------------
- ☐ ----------------------------------
- ☐ ----------------------------------
- ☐ ----------------------------------
- ☐ ----------------------------------
- ☐ ----------------------------------

NOTES

REMINDER

TO DO LIST

MONTH ....   DATE ....

TO DO

- [ ] ....
- [ ] ....
- [ ] ....
- [ ] ....
- [ ] ....
- [ ] ....
- [ ] ....
- [ ] ....
- [ ] ....
- [ ] ....
- [ ] ....
- [ ] ....
- [ ] ....
- [ ] ....
- [ ] ....
- [ ] ....
- [ ] ....
- [ ] ....
- [ ] ....
- [ ] ....
- [ ] ....
- [ ] ....
- [ ] ....
- [ ] ....
- [ ] ....

PRIORITIES

- [ ] ....
- [ ] ....
- [ ] ....
- [ ] ....
- [ ] ....
- [ ] ....
- [ ] ....

NOTES

REMINDER

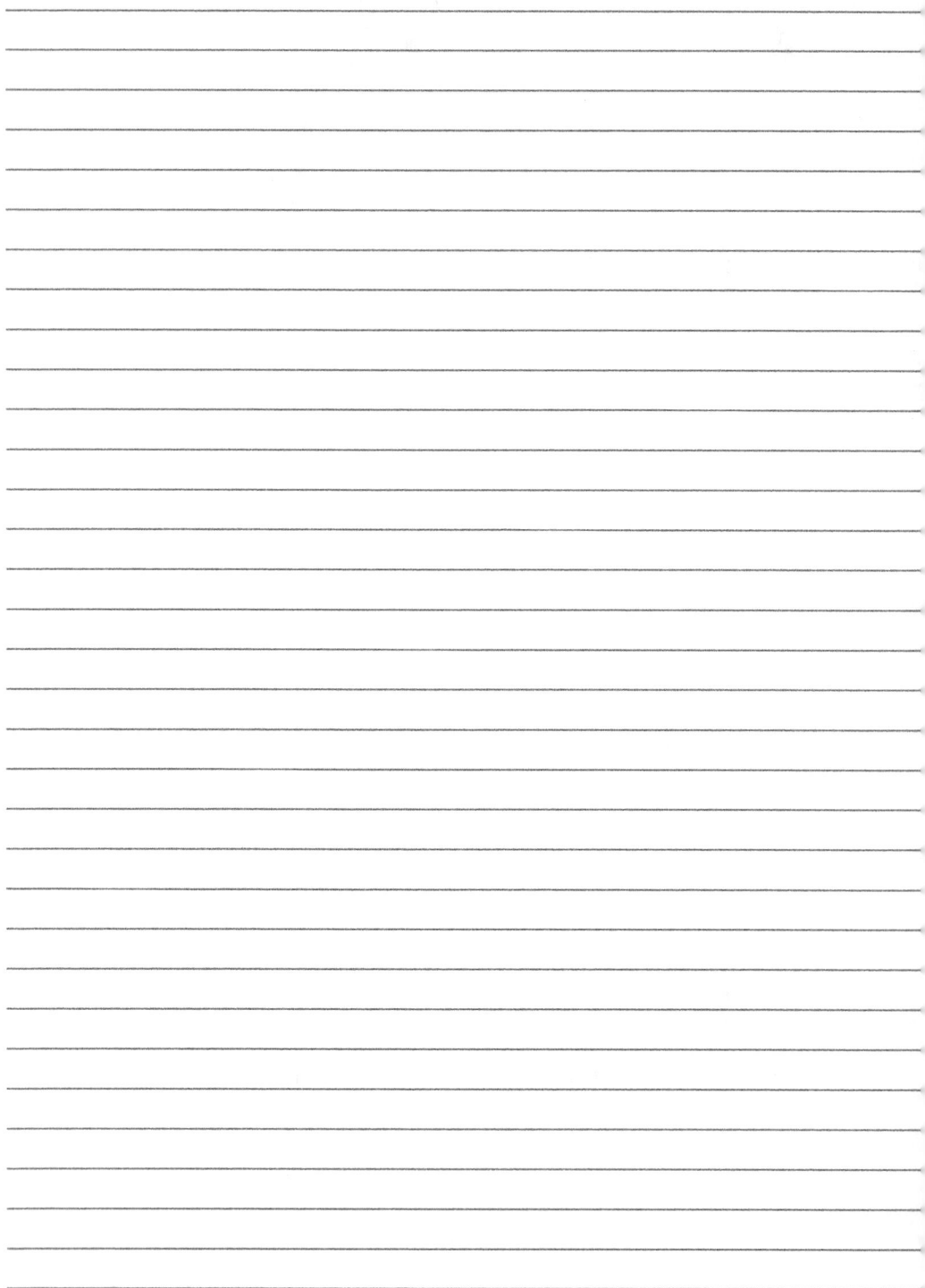

www.ingramcontent.com/pod-product-compliance
Lightning Source LLC
Chambersburg PA
CBHW060236030426
42335CB00014B/1479